GOOD ❖ OLD ❖ DAYS®

Live It Again™

1949

TRUMAN
JOHN FALTER

Dear Friends,

Mobility was the name of the game as 1949 "the last year of the 1940s" dawned.

Americans were more mobile than ever. With families literally bursting at the seams with Baby Boom births, we were looking for new homes and, often, new hometowns. We were moving places where there were better jobs, better schools and better living conditions.

After his surprise victory and reelection in November 1948, Harry Truman launched his Fair Deal movement to help a burgeoning economy prepare for the Fabulous Fifties. Better roads meant easier transportation, and "long haul trucking" was added to our vocabulary. Bigger and more durable trucks moved every conceivable product "yes, even households" across the city, across the state and across the nation.

Harry Truman launched his Fair Deal movement to help a burgeoning economy prepare for the Fabulous Fifties.

Families were upwardly mobile as well. A strong economy was fueling the job market and those jobs were paying better for both men and women. Women particularly were finding their way into better and more diverse occupations. They had gained valuable experience while filling the job void during World War II. Now they were making "two income families" a familiar phrase.

Mobility meant prosperity and prosperity seemed to be everywhere as the 1940s were nearing the end. It was 1949, and it was great to be young and alive!

Contents

1949 PAN AMERICAN

1949 PONTIAC

1949 TRAILER COACH MANUFACTURERS ASSOCIATION

1949 ARIVN'S

Everyday Life

Around the neighborhood

The local church proved to be the glue of neighborhood life. Many people whose lives were committed to the religious community were baptized, married and eventually eulogized through the same local worship nucleus. Neighbors often caught up on the week's activities while chatting with each other following Sunday services. Primary social gatherings were church fellowship groups and weekly activities for various community interests.

The church facility was also utilized for such organizations as scouts and children's clubs. Voting and neighborhood interest meetings were often held at the community church. A sense of warmth and home often permeated the hearts of those who had spent their entire lives as members of the local congregation.

Neighborhood entertainment was often found in watching building projects or changes going on in the properties of those who lived nearby.

The elderly often found their greatest joy in greeting and visiting with the neighborhood children. Youngsters learned some of life's simplest lessons by observing the lives of the older people around them.

"He's so proud of that whistle that people can't hear, I'd hate for him to know that I can't hear it either!"

Everyday Life

Local heroes

Young people looked up to firemen, policemen, local public officials and teachers so much, that they would stop in their tracks in awe when they showed up on the scene. Children loved wearing toy firemen gear, police caps and badges.

It was a time when heroes were present in the lives of children to the extent that many young people had desires to become policemen or firemen when they grew up.

A caring hug from a local policeman or the presence of firemen and other public safety officials brought awe and respect to children and youth who appreciated local heroes.

"Perhaps they don't want your advice, Henry."

The Metro Daily News
FINAL EDITION
JANUARY 5, 1949
PRESIDENT TRUMAN UNVEILS "FAIR DEAL" PROGRAM

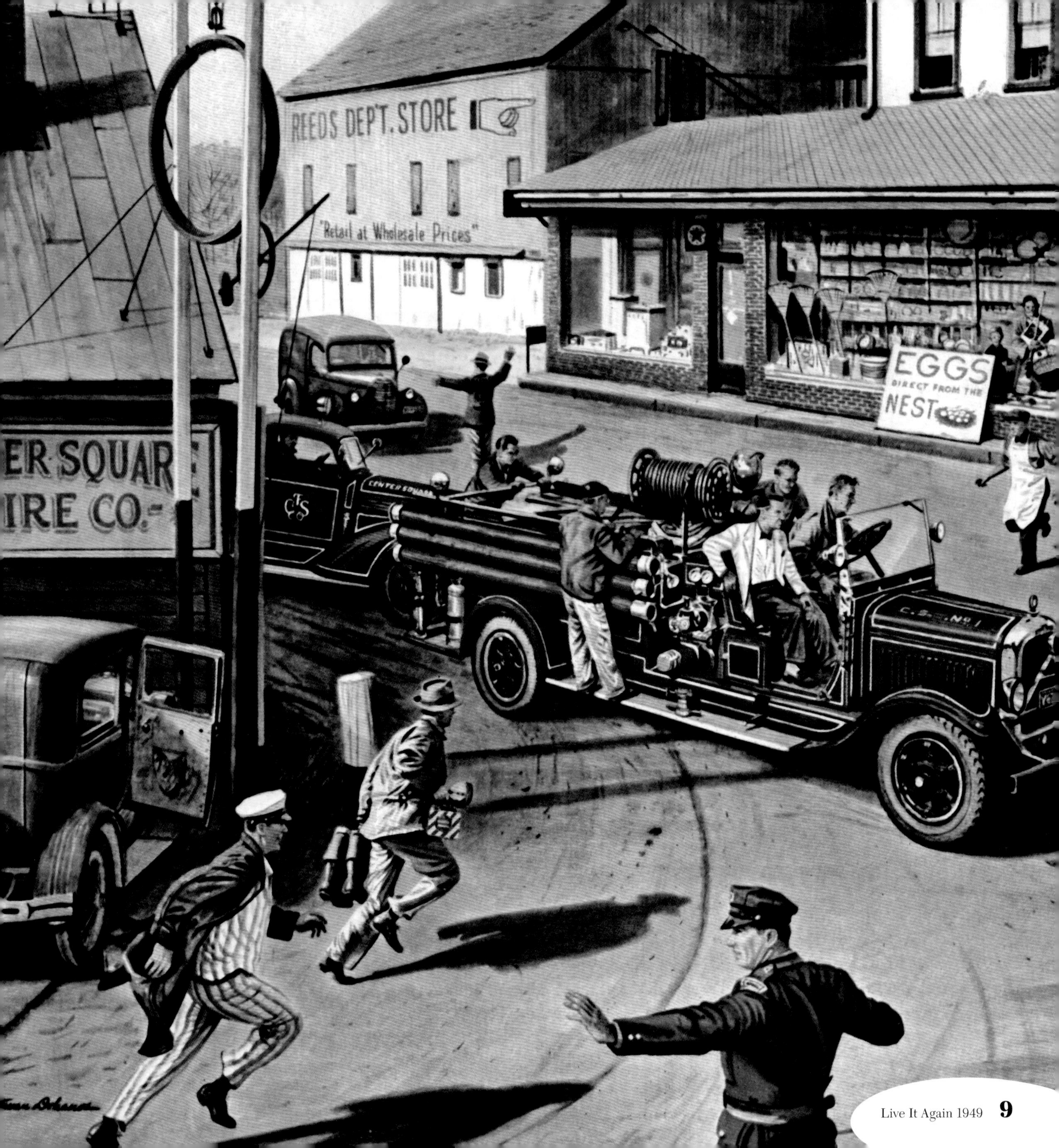
REEDS DEPT. STORE
"Retail at Wholesale Prices"
ER SQUARE
IRE CO.
EGGS
DIRECT FROM THE
NEST
C.S. No 1

FAMOUS BIRTHDAYS

John Slobodnik, January 1
artist

George Foreman, January 10
prize fighter

Everyday Life

Around town

Those who installed the first television in the community were sure to find visitors on their doorsteps who were curious about viewing and the operation of the TV set. Owners who were sociable would often invite neighbors to watch some of the first entertainment and sports productions. The item of most interest often was what certain people really looked like. Up until that time, listeners were forced to use their imagination concerning the appearance of those they heard on the radio. The actual appearance of the program stars always created great interest.

For many, the technology involved in connecting the television to the antenna was just as fascinating. Neighbors gathered to watch as television owners attached the wires of their set to the antenna.

1949 AMERICAN AIRLINES

© 1949 SEPS

"Where'd you get that carrot?"

1949 GULFPRIDE OIL

Another facet of small town life that was enjoyed by those who were extremely social was the friendship acquired through mailmen or the doorman at local hotels or hospitals. Conversations based on first names were part of the social fabric of those who had lived for an extended period of time in the local community.

REPRINTED WITH PERMISSION FROM ALCOA

Public figures, such as policemen and mailmen, were viewed as community friends who often took the time to visit or share the latest news with town residents.

Everyday Life

Baby boom

The return of soldiers from World War II brought a quick change in family and population growth. More marriages meant more children which brought about new demands in health care and food chain expectations. Clothing businesses flourished and the housing industry increased rapidly. As the children grew into adulthood, the nation was faced with an entire cultural change demanding more employment and larger schools. More children meant the need for more teachers and opportunities for athletic and skill development.

REPRINTED WITH PERMISSION FROM MONSANTO CHEMICALS & PLASTICS

Growth in the number of children following World War II brought a greater need in the health care field. Improved technology led to more advanced care for the newborn.

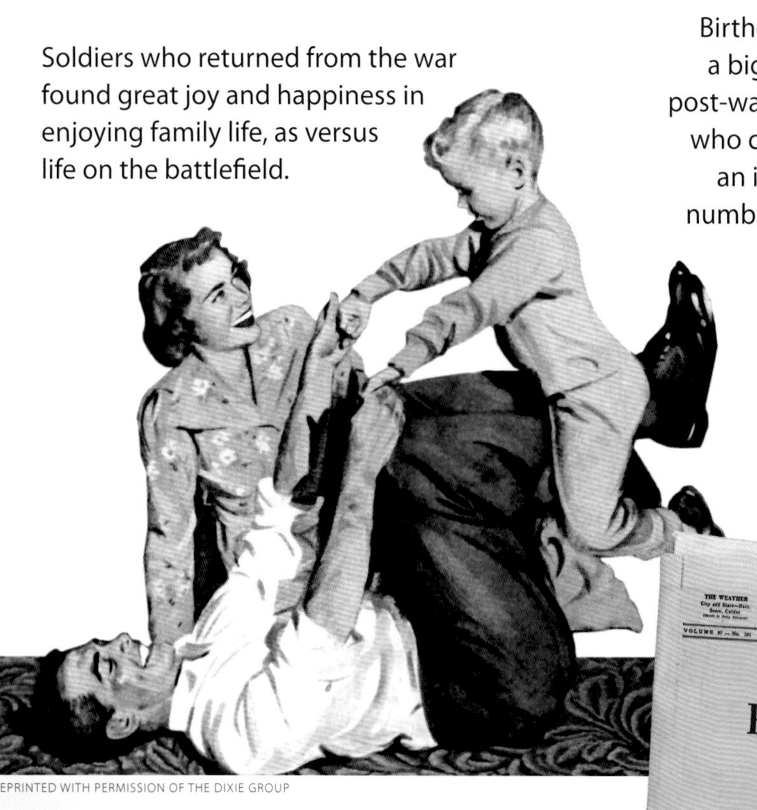

Soldiers who returned from the war found great joy and happiness in enjoying family life, as versus life on the battlefield.

REPRINTED WITH PERMISSION OF THE DIXIE GROUP

Birthdays were a big thing for post-war families, who celebrated an increasing number of child births.

1949 PAN AMERICAN COFFEE BUREAU

The Metro Daily News FINAL EDITION

JANUARY 25, 1949

FIRST EMMY AWARDS PRESENTED

This gala event was held at the Hollywood Athletic Club.

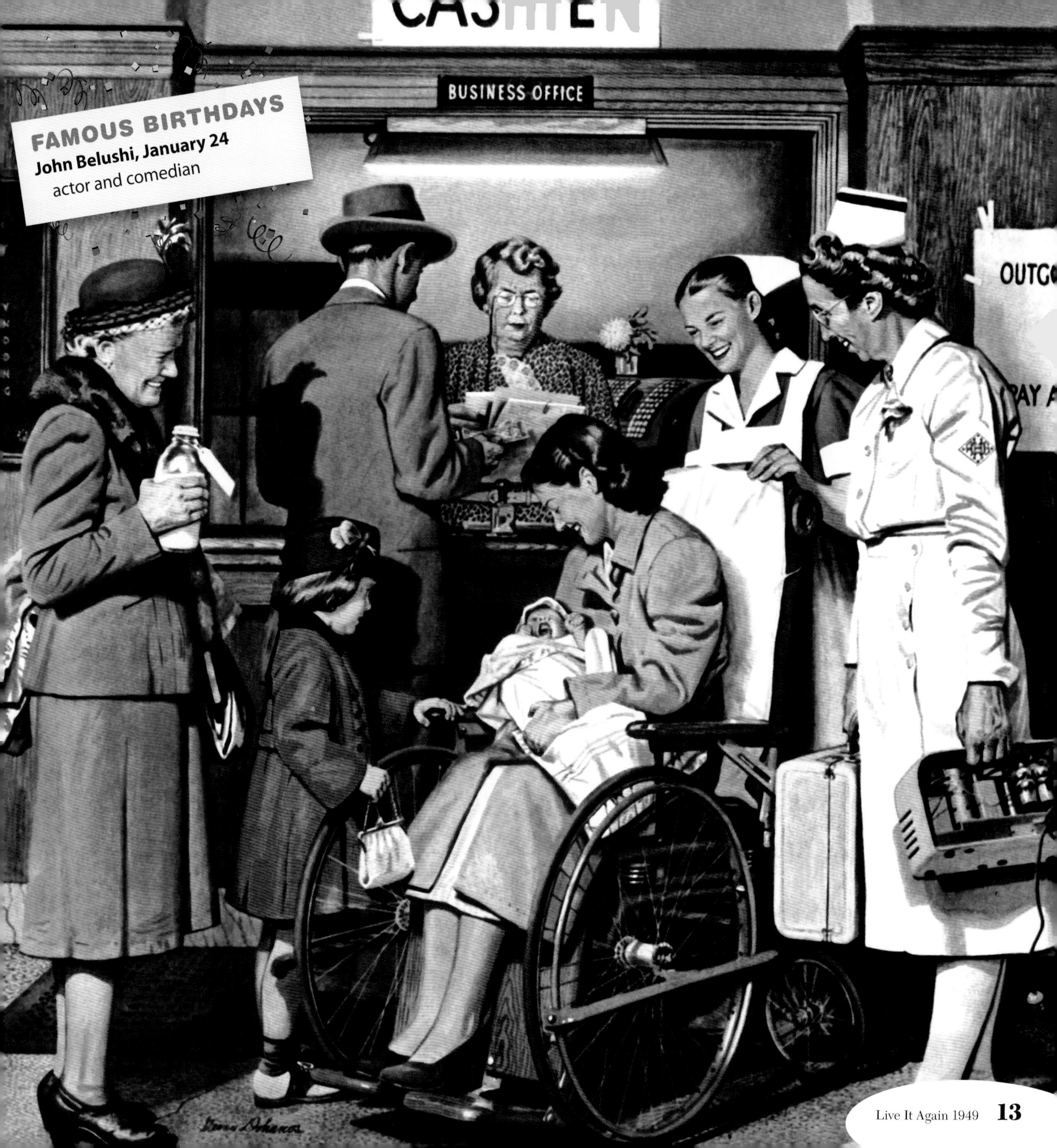

FAMOUS BIRTHDAYS

John Belushi, January 24
actor and comedian

Learning to do chores was often a working and enjoyable time together. Children often learned responsibilities while talking over life's events with family members.

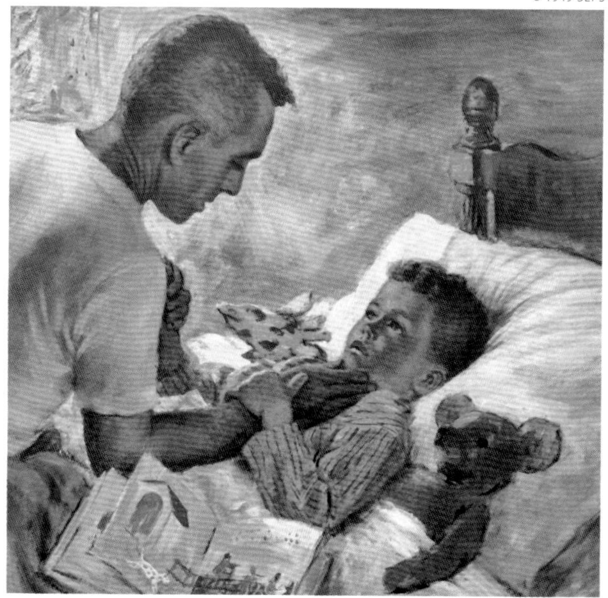

Bedtime stories were an important time of connecting with parents as well as learning to appreciate reading. Children loved to pick out new storybooks to share during this quality time with Mom or Dad.

Families loved to window shop together with dreams of sometime owning the items being viewed. Families often walked past department stores, checking out sale products in the window, and then ending up with a special snack somewhere.

Gathering to play games while enjoying snacks, such as popcorn or homemade baked goods, was a favorite evening pastime. Often, friends would invite others over for an evening of activities. Sometimes everyone would get involved in the games and other times adults would visit while children played such games as Old Maid and Monopoly.

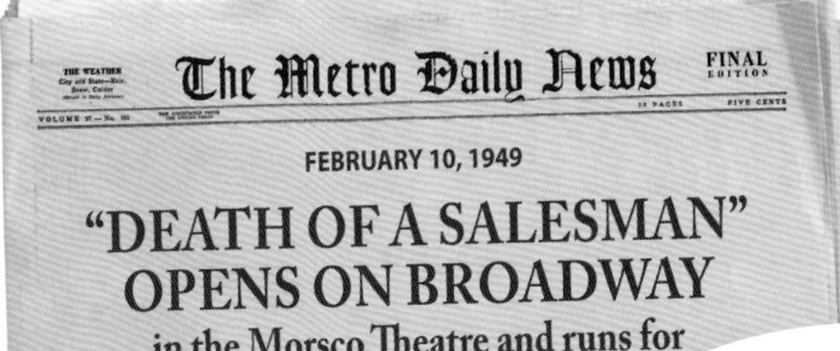

The Metro Daily News

FINAL EDITION

FEBRUARY 10, 1949

"DEATH OF A SALESMAN" OPENS ON BROADWAY

in the Morsco Theatre and runs for 742 performances.

What Made Us Laugh

"A salesman got through once, but by the time he reached the door he was too weak to talk."

"This is fun. How come you don't take us fishing more often?"

"Well, I had in mind some sort of a policy that would enable me to retire right now."

"Who locked the piano?"

"Look, mommy, I found my drum, and my bugle, and the police whistle I lost, and ..."

"Remember, you're my guest. If you say you don't go to bed till ten o'clock, their hands are tied."

"You can see she's against me—she has me even dumber than I was last month and you know that's impossible!"

NATIONAL PARK SERVICE, ABBIE ROWE, COURTESY OF HARRY S. TRUMAN LIBRARY

A Year With the President

Not many political analysts had anticipated that Harry Truman would be making the presidential inaugural speech in 1949. Many felt that Truman, who had stepped into the shoes of Franklin D. Roosevelt after he died just three months into his third term, would fall to popular Republican Thomas Dewey. However Truman won and continued to lead the nation in efforts to contain communism and the Cold War.

The tough talking president was especially famous for his well-known statements "The buck stops here" and "If you can't stand the heat, get out of the kitchen." With his election for a second term, Truman sought to direct peace efforts in Europe while giving new direction to a postwar economy. To help the burgeoning economy, Truman launched his Fair Deal movement.

NATIONAL PARK SERVICE, ABBIE ROWE, COURTESY OF HARRY S. TRUMAN LIBRARY

COPYRIGHT UNKNOWN, COURTESY OF HARRY S. TRUMAN LIBRARY

NATIONAL PARK SERVICE, ABBIE ROWE, COURTESY OF HARRY S. TRUMAN LIBRARY

President Harry Truman gives the inauguration speech introducing his second term. Many felt that Truman would be defeated by Thomas Dewey in the presidential election, but a popular whistle-stop tour lifted the incumbant over the top as the post-World War II chief executive.

U.S. ARMY, COURTESY OF HARRY S. TRUMAN LIBRARY

COPYRIGHT UNKNOWN, COURTESY OF HARRY S. TRUMAN LIBRARY

President Harry Truman and Vice President Alben Barkley wave with confidence as they walk out of the White House on their way to the presidential reviewing stand for the 1949 inauguration.

In February, the Lone Ranger, played by Clayton Moore, and his sidekick Tonto, played by Jay Silverheels, became one of the first famed radio programs to make a television debut.

Television

Television was still in its infancy. Shows such as *The Lone Ranger* and *The Life of Riley* were making their debut. Arthur Godfrey also introduced a show, *Arthur Godfrey and His Friends*, that would be broadcast for the next decade.

The technical aspects of television broadcasting continued to advance as a two-hour special celebrated the linking of the eastern and midwestern networks and RCA announced the development of a compatible color TV system.

In many neighborhoods, only one or two individuals could afford television. Quite often, their home would become sites of gathering neighbors with plenty of popcorn to watch their favorite show in a theater-like atmosphere.

© GETTY IMAGES

Martin Kane, Private Eye was the first detective show aired on television. Terror occurred when the blonde actress clubbed the star of the show after she discovered he hid the loot.

FAMOUS BIRTHDAYS

Niki Lauda, February 22

Austrian race car driver

© GETTY IMAGES

Buffalo Bob and his puppet sidekick, Howdy Doody, made their way into the world of children through the introduction of the popular, *Howdy Doody* show. Children often hastened home from school to watch Buffalo Bob and his friends along with its famous theme song "It's Howdy Doody Time."

1949 GENERAL ELECTRIC COMPANY

Television

Which model to buy?

The coming of television opened a new field of marketing competition. Initially, viewing was mainly possible after dark. However, General Electric, one of the first on the market, quickly focused on screen brightness that could be observed during both day and night. Advertising of the time indicated that GE viewing was possible all day and in a fully lighted room. RCA Victor responded with a television that boasted an automatic station selector. RCA also emphasized more steady pictures and less rolling of static.

One of the initial problems with early television was interference of stations which resulted in static and periodic snowy pictures. Therefore, the slogan accompanying Admiral televisions was "clearest picture of all." Competitive style and design became more of an issue as televisions were soon created to blend in with other furniture styles of the day.

© 1949 SEPS

"This one is for short wave and FM, that's the recorder, and that's the television; this other one is the two-speed record changer, and this thing is good if you have any of those old player-piano rolls left."

1949 GENERAL ELECTRIC COMPANY

At first, television viewing was mainly possible after dark. Quickly, competing companies fought to demonstrate the sharpest and clearest picture during daylight and in lighted rooms.

1949 GENERAL ELECTRIC COMPANY

REPRINTED WITH PERMISSION OF TECHNICOLOR

In the war for best daytime television, GE advertised as being "80 percent brighter" than competing companies. The ability to watch TV all day quickly brought out the possibility of soap operas, daytime talk and game shows. Table-model style soon caught the fancy of those seeking to compete with having the best television in the neighborhood.

1949 GENERAL ELECTRIC COMPANY

1949 ADMIRAL

The combination of television and record player case intrigued many, especially the wealthy. Soon, the cost of console televisions dropped, making them affordable and attractive for average middle-class individuals.

Home Style

© LIBRARY OF CONGRESS, PRINTS AND PHOTOGRAPHS DIVISION, GSC 5A16366

Once the war was over, manufacturing emphasis could shift from making war supplies to domestic items for home and family. Many people who put house repairs on hold during the war found immediate postwar times to be an excellent opportunity to bring a new look to their homes.

Many did their own redecorating; for some, it provided an opportunity to gather as family and friends. Redecorating chores such as wall papering, changing rooms around or putting in new closets often brought opportunities to visit and eat along the way. Sometimes, such working gatherings were also a good opportunity to share new snacks. Often, those who worked together in one home, moved on to other homes as a decorating team.

© LIBRARY OF CONGRESS, PRINTS AND PHOTOGRAPHS DIVISION, GSC 5A16361

© 1949 SEPS

"I'd like to paint your house. This is a sample of my work."

REPRINTED WITH PERMISSION FROM NATIONAL GYPSUM COMPANY

The trend to combine family lounges with guest bedrooms provided a relaxing spot to read or take a daytime nap.

The Metro Daily News

FINAL EDITION

MARCH 2, 1949

B-50 SUPER FORTRESS "LUCKY LADY II" COMPLETES THE FIRST NON-STOP AROUND-THE-WORLD FLIGHT

It was refueled four times in the air.

More convenient items allowed quicker assistance in preparing family members to leave for the day's activities. White enameled steel was the in-thing in many kitchen decors. "Touch convenience" sold modern kitchens to many families.

1949 YOUNGSTOWN KITCHENS

The idea of gas water heaters brought convenience in washing dishes and opportunities for modern clothes washing machines. Previously, water was often heated in pans on kitchen stoves and poured into dish pans to wash the dishes from each meal.

REPRINTED WITH PERMISSION OF THE AMERICAN GAS ASSOCIATION

FAMOUS BIRTHDAYS

Vicki Lawrence, March 26
comedienne and game show hostess

Home Style

The concept of a modern kitchen combined style and convenience. Arrangement of shelves and sinks to speed up the washing and filing of utensils and plates became more popular. Single cabinets and the use of dishpans to do dishes were replaced by built-in cabinets surrounding a modern sink. All of this was promoted to allow mothers to spend more time with children and family members to have shorter waiting periods in receiving their meals. This new style also made it easier for children to help with kitchen chores.

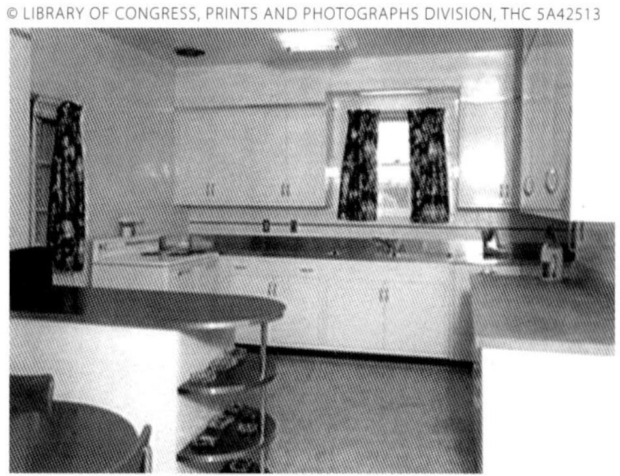

A stove on one side of the kitchen sink and a refrigerator on the other were symbolic of fewer steps and quicker production in accomplishing kitchen tasks.

Modern Conveniences

Cooking

The manufacturing of such conveniences as toasters and modern mixers made life much easier. Large appliances such as gas ranges and chest and upright freezers all made cooking and food storage much more simple. Prior to the affordability of home freezers, families often rented frozen food locker storage to preserve garden vegetables.

Waffle irons, space heaters and clothes irons also became more affordable and convenient to those in charge of household chores.

1949 SUNBEAM

The multiple tasks performed by Sunbean Mixmasters gave numerous options with one appliance.

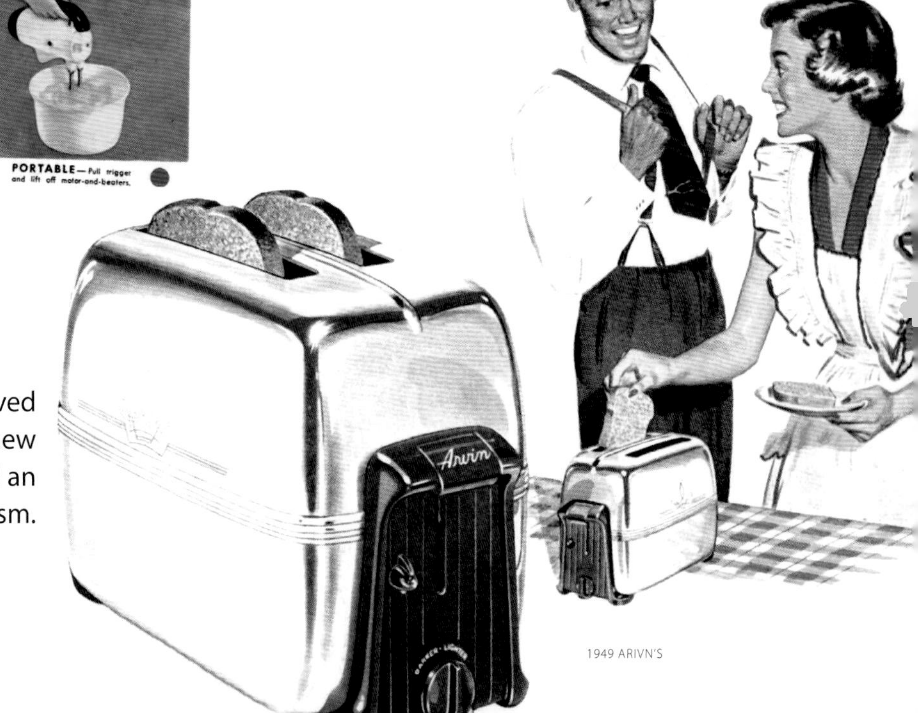

The coming of automatic toasters improved the quality of the product with such new additions as strategic selectors and an automatic pop-up mechanism.

1949 ARIVN'S

Convenience was at it's best for the consumer. Just the thought of an electric icebox was exciting to any homeowner. Ice cream could be kept frozen while lettuce stayed cool and crisp.

1949 COOLERATOR

Gas ranges were marketed as an easy appliance to use without a lot of new cooking rules, or misunderstood gadgets. One selling point was the fact that they continued to function even if electricity was shut down by a winter storm.

alajálov.

Modern Conveniences

Cleaning

The idea of doing dishes without washing them in the sink introduced a whole new era of cleaning convenience to busy homemakers. Hot Point dishwashers were simple enough to be loaded by children while Westinghouse automatic washing machines presented an entire new challenge in proper laundry cleaning.

The fact that new cleaning appliances were less complicated, assisted mothers with keeping the household clean and orderly.

The Westinghouse Laundromat was advertised as being completely automatic and carrying the ability to make clothes whiter than old-fashioned hand washing.

"It seems too good to be true. They've played in the house all day and haven't broken a thing."

Automatic dishwashers such as this Hotpoint model were so simple to operate that even children could load and unload them.

What Made Us Laugh

"You should have been here ten years ago!"

"There, it's all ready to be knocked over."

"They must breed like flies.
Twenty years ago you seldom saw one."

"He says the answer is no—but he thanked me for my interest."

"Why am I here? What does all this mean in the infinite scheme of things?"

"No, no, dear! I left our car for an oil change and Mr. Woods is just dropping me off on his way to take that old wreck to the junkyard."

"That's all there is—but it's very effective,"

"He's got your eyes."

1949 JEEP

Trucks

Around the neighborhood

Growing production of trucks introduced the convenience of transporting in pickups instead of trying to squeeze things into the trunk of the family car. Trucks also became a status symbol of young drivers and adults who still had a bit of youthful zeal in them. While many city individuals liked to polish their truck and show it off, the use of trucks in rural and farm settings took on more practical meaning. Trucks were used to haul things around on the farm while many young truck drivers drove around town in their vehicle that would quickly become outmoded.

1949 STUDEBAKER

Studebaker trucks quickly became popular for those wishing to portray style and youthful zeal.

The Metro Daily News

FINAL EDITION

APRIL 4, 1949

NORTH ATLANTIC TREATY SIGNED IN WASHINGTON D.C., CREATING THE NATO DEFENSE ALLIANCE

Lessons
PEPIES
PEPIES
PEPIES
PEPIES
Nº532
33974
Norman
Rockwell

Two-speed axles contributed to the engine wear and saved time and fuel in steep driving.

Those trucks hauling large loads specialized in cabin-over-engine chassis. A six-wheel chassis proved effective in carrying such heavy loads as logs.

Trucks

Across the country

The improved durability of truck suspension and bed construction allowed American truckers to increase load size and road miles in transporting industrial needs across the country. Axles, transmissions and frames were all strengthened to handle harsh and long-lasting road wear.

Trucks that proved to haul the biggest and longest loads became the brand names of choice for the trucking industry. Truckers were committed to maintaining 24-hour service in delivering industrial products from one part of the country to the other. Improved roads and a greater supply of gasoline added to the industry's proficiency.

1949 FRUEHAUF

Trucks, such as this one by Fruehauf, were often used to move parts and supplies between main plants and warehouses. Many such trucks were on the road for at least two shifts.

REPRINTED COURTESY OF EATON CORPORATION

Trucks such as this Eaton were used to deliver acids and other liquids. The trucks enabled buyers to receive shipments on short notice when they needed them, reducing the need for storing.

The Metro Daily News

FINAL EDITION

APRIL 18, 1949

EIRE LEAVES THE BRITISH COMMONWEALTH AND BECOMES THE REPUBLIC OF IRELAND

1949 STUDEBAKER

1949 STUDEBAKER

Keeping America Running

Thousands of workers took to the poles in all kinds of weather to make sure that America's power and telephone service continued to perform without interruption. Maintaining millions of miles of wire and cable was no easy task. When interruptions did occur, workers were faced with the grueling job of locating the problem and repairing it. The reliability of those maintaining the nation's grid was a matter of trust and commitment.

Other professional craftsmen were in charge of assuring that the country's cars, trucks and farm machinery ran smoothly over many miles of roads and agricultural fields.

Industrial technology increased rapidly following the war. As the nation turned from weapon production to improvement of the domestic industry, maintenance jobs became a prime source of employment for an economy coming back.

FAMOUS BIRTHDAYS

John Oates, April 7 rock singer and guitarist of Hall & Oates

Jessica Lange, April 20 actress

What Made Us Laugh

"Sure, you used to get one hundred in history … there wasn't much to remember then!"

"We're so proud of him—we've never hadda musician in the family before."

"He writes us every week—even if it's only for five or six dollars."

"Mr. Fosdick? There's a lot of birthday cards in your wife's mail this morning—I thought you ought to know!"

Everyday Life

Women at work

During the war, women filled in work positions that had been traditionally filled by men. When military personnel returned to the workforce, it meant the creation of new jobs for returning soldiers. Many women found out they enjoyed being a part of the workforce and decided to continue working outside the home.

The acceptance of women into the workforce was a new step in perception of gender responsibilities. The idea of "male jobs" and "female jobs" was still prevalent in many regions. Female employment had generally been perceived as medical and educational fields, while men were perceived as leaders in white collar and heavy work in blue-collar employment.

During the war, women proved themselves to be capable and even superior in many job performances, thus starting a new trend that would change the role of women in the workforce forever.

Women continued being employed outside the home even after the boys were home from war. Many women found they enjoyed making their own money.

Women were taking on new roles in the workforce. Many of them were working side by side with men in white collar jobs.

Many women continued to work as nurses, having hearts of compassion for those who were suffering.

1949 WESTERN ELECTRIC

The technological advances in communication opened up many jobs for women, especially as switchboard operators for the local telephone company.

© 1949 SEPS

"So you're Mr. J. M. Twiddle. I've filed you away hundreds of times."

COURTESY OF UNISYS CORPORATION

New streetlights in the neighborhood created an atmosphere that was more safe and proper for walking longer distances after dark. It was all part of a bustling world coming to life with new prosperity following the more dismal days of the Great Depression and World War II.

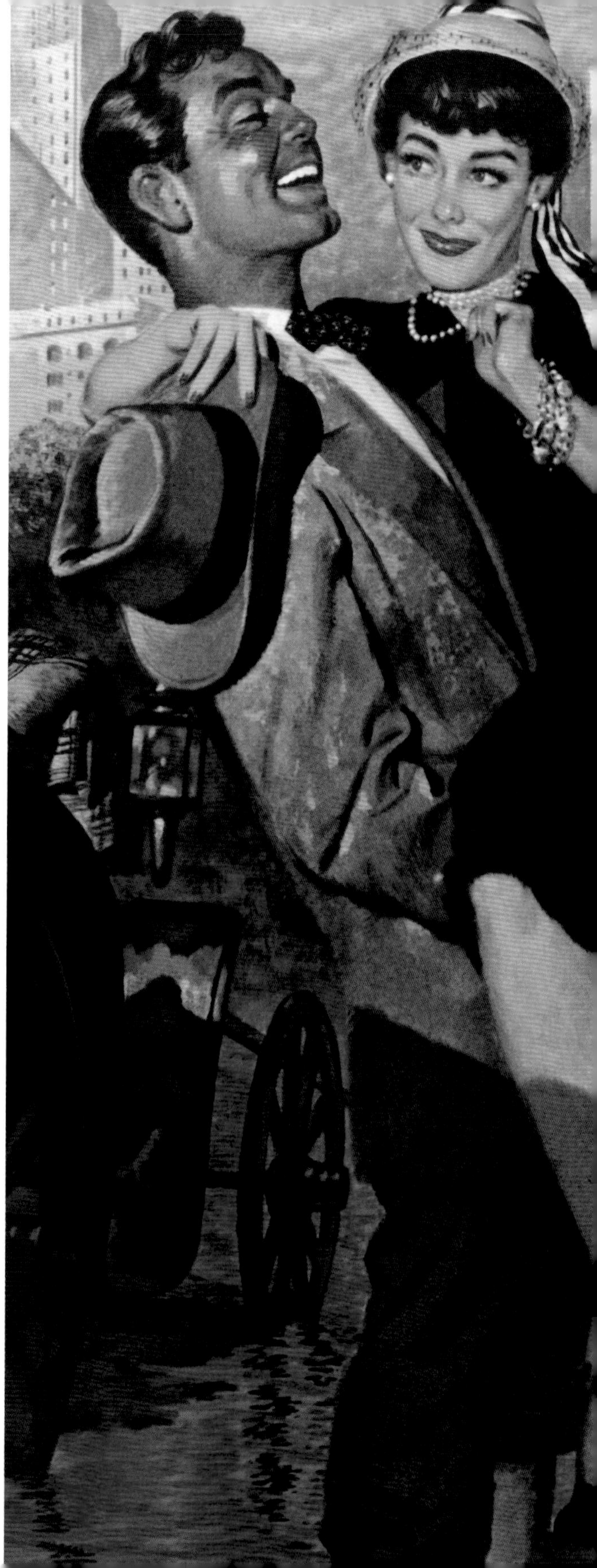

The City After Dark

Moonlight and reflections of city lights dancing on the water made for romantic and passionate evenings for lovers. Dress for nightlife was also very special with gowns and formal wear creating an atmosphere of warmth for those sharing formal meals and dancing during a night out on the town.

The growing provision of athletic field lights and other illuminated facilities created potential for family outings and community events after the sun went down.

Women of Intrigue

Many of the soldiers that had returned from World War II went through difficult times adjusting back into American mainstream life, and dealing with memories and flashbacks of war experiences. Some had lost girlfriends to other relationships, and others were seeking new relationships and a new way of life.

Many women who felt deeply for men in the military sought to provide love and encouragement while trying to understand their feelings of hurt. As soldiers attempted to develop relationships and settle back into a sociable lifestyle, women sought to process and understand their wounded spirits.

Women gave looks of intrigue with searching eyes as they sought to be there for returning military personnel who returned home confused and in need of understanding.

A woman appears to give a look of contemplation in response to words spoken by a soldier. It often took much understanding to help those seeking to restore their ways back into mainstream living.

A mystical but very intense look on the face of this woman reflects the special bond of concentration in seeking to understand the heart of the man.

Pinstripe shirts and a more casual look led the way in a nation searching for new designs.

FAMOUS BIRTHDAYS

Billy Joel, May 9
singer–songwriter and pianist

Hank Williams Jr., May 26
country singer

Men's Fashion

Following the war, most men were tired of uniforms and restrictions. When they returned home, many men preferred generously cut suits of herringbone or special plaid fabrics.

Pinstripe suits quickly led the way in fashion changes that continued to dominate thoughts of more casualness and comfortable lifestyle. Ties were generally short and very colorful. There was a large variety in tie designs, many of them were bold and bright in color.

1949 HABAND COMPANY

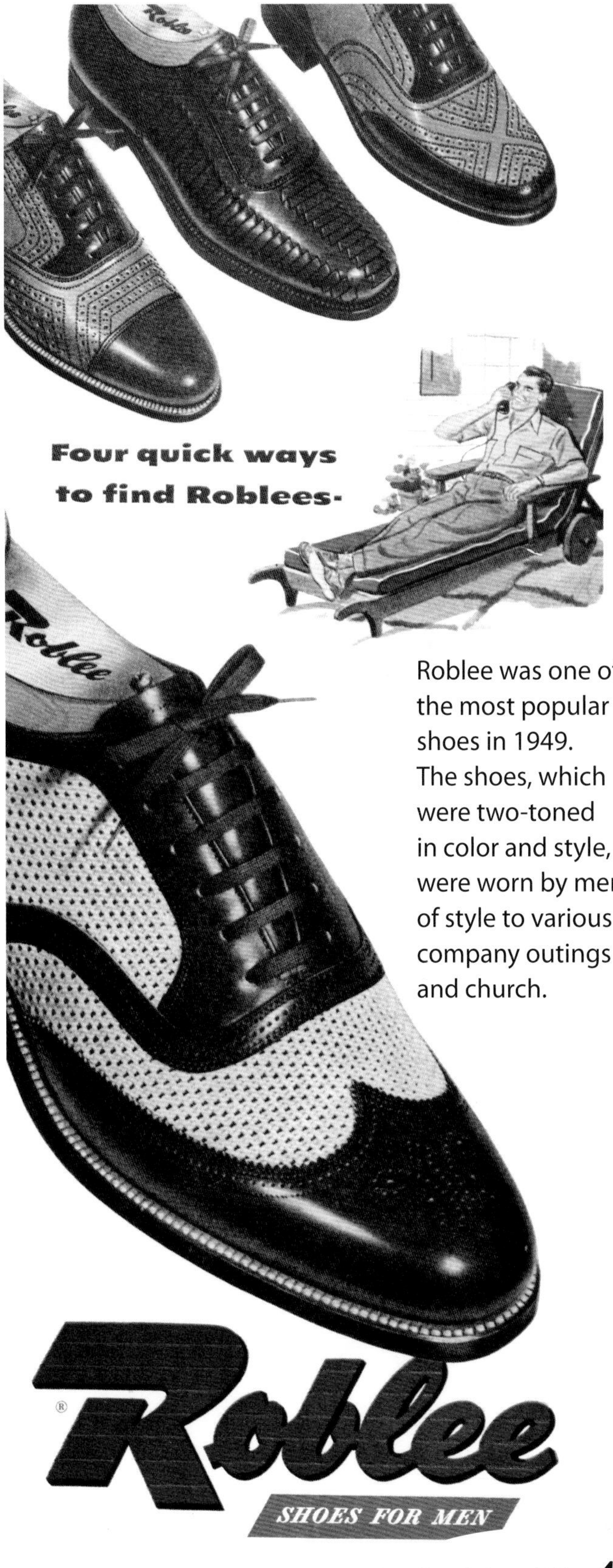

Four quick ways to find Roblees-

Roblee

® Roblee

SHOES FOR MEN

1949 ROBLEE

Roblee was one of the most popular shoes in 1949. The shoes, which were two-toned in color and style, were worn by men of style to various company outings and church.

Hats

The ultimate accessory

A sharp-looking hat was considered the crowning mark of distinction for both men and women. Hat fashions expanded after the war years in both make and size. Both straw and felt hats were acceptable for men, while ladies' hats for the year were divided sharply into very small hats or very large hats.

As always, hat-wear reached its peak of emphasis on Easter Sunday, with small-brimmed sailors, flowered bonnets and big-brimmed hats. A woman wasn't dressed at her best unless she had the perfect hat to match her outfit.

Hats varied greatly in size and design, with straw hats considered the style for summer wear while velour and velvets in pastel or rich deep colors were the leading style of choice for winter.

"Coats go on the bed—I take care of the hats."

The smaller head-capping hats were designed to complement the generally accepted short-hair coiffure. Pillbox hats were worn straight on the head while small cap-like silhouettes were usually worn with a tilt to one side.

What Made Us Laugh

"I don't want to break your wagon, Jack, but she's getting seventy-five cents an hour to sit for me."

"Gosh, I didn't think we'd ever go home—did you?"

"The express will be by in ten minutes, but I advise you to wait for the local … it stops."

"No thanks, I just came in to load my camera."

“Oh, I suppose I did complain too much about my sandwiches falling apart, but …”

“Why, I have always understood from Billy here that you have four children.”

“The Penrose will is something of a surprise. Take a number.”

“Be with you in a moment. Make yourself comfortable.”

Everyday Life

Relaxing outdoors

Outdoor relaxation often involved water activities. For some, it was securing a lake cottage by some resort. Others preferred to pack the family picnic basket with sandwiches and freshly picked fruit and head toward a park along a tranquil flowing river. Many began to purchase lawn furniture that could be transported so that adults could read and visit while children splashed in the water.

Fishing outings were always popular. The upgrading of equipment to cast rods introduced a new art to avid fishermen attempting to display their talents to their children. Many ocean beaches developed amusement parks to attract families, not only for the day, but for vacation time at their resort hotels.

Hats were still a part of recreational activities, with straw hats becoming more popular for outside activities involving the men.

Dress styles had become less formal, but only in the sense of sleeveless dresses. Many still wore jewelry even to recreational activities. Guys often wore long-sleeved shirts to protect themselves from the heat.

The Metro Daily News

FINAL EDITION

JUNE 8, 1949

GEORGE ORWELL'S BOOK *1984* IS PUBLISHED

JOHN FALTER

John Clymer

Everyday Life

On the farm

Farm life proved to be a natural environment for developing a sense of community and learning responsibility. Children followed their parents to the garden with hoes and sprinkling cans. Girls worked in the kitchen helping their mothers bake and cook for hungry farmhands. Young boys made heroes of the men and sought to follow in their footsteps.

During the annual agricultural show, farm youth exhibited projects of livestock and vegetables representing hard work in their rural surroundings. Farmers gathered and compared crops and farm prices. Often they exchanged new ideas for farming techniques.

FAMOUS BIRTHDAYS
Meryl Streep, June 22
actress

Youth and adults alike worked together in maintaining farm property. No one was exempt from contributing to a day's work regardless of age or gender.

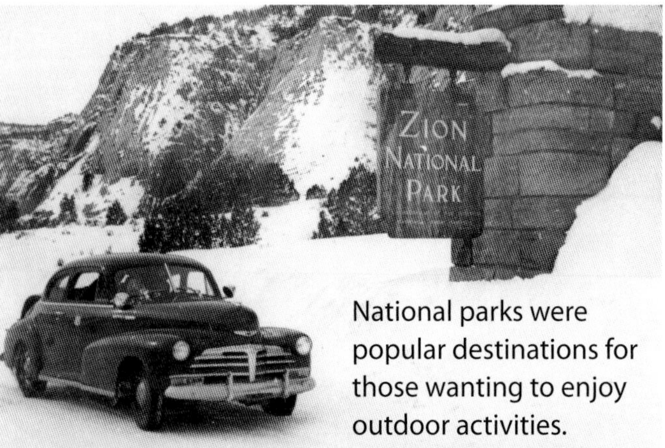

National parks were popular destinations for those wanting to enjoy outdoor activities.

The Great Outdoors

Improved transportation made it possible to travel to scenic sites and relaxation areas that were once considered only for the elite. Family vacations to national parks and outdoor resorts became more common as children and parents enjoyed fishing and hiking together. In the evenings, back at their cabins, everyone would join in playing card games, board games and enjoying tales of family history.

Paved highways made places accessible that were once considered to be a long distance away. Getting out to see outdoor scenery became a treat for those who had been confined to their local area for most of their lives.

Fees were charged at gatehouse entries into the parks. The money was used for park maintenance and development.

Campfires were cozy places to visit to enjoy roasted hot dogs and sometimes listen to the quiet and relaxing sounds of nature.

Camping, fishing and enjoying outdoors drew people together. There wasn't a stranger among those who shared the common bond of land and recreational interests.

Developing trailer parks became a rapidly rising business to accommodate this consistently growing industry. Parks were considered a good investment. Many of them included swimming pools and beaches.

1949 TRAILER COACH MANUFACTURERS ASSOCIATION

© 1949 SEPS

"I wish we could afford a car.
I'm tired of living with other people!"

Various companies began competing for sales rights in marketing mobile homes. Companies advertised such relatively new assets as cozy warmth and cross-summer ventilation.

1949 SCHULT

Mobile Home Living

The increased popularity of trailer parks offered a new recreational opportunity for family experiences. Many people were attracted to outdoor parks that provided close contact with nature.

The new trailers of the time included living rooms, separate bedrooms and modern equipped kitchens. Shower and good toilet facilities rounded out the hominess of the latest model trailers which were equipped with plenty of ventilation for summer leisure or warm heat for winter outings.

1949 PALACE CORPORATION

Mobile living was designed with warmth for home living. Families developed the atmosphere of home that provided for all of the dynamics they enjoyed in their primary home.

1949 PALACE CORPORATION

© 1949 SEPS

"I told you not to nail down the carpet!"

Summer Fun

On the water

The mischief that could be created by a group of young boys was always interesting. One favorite activity was climbing trees and jumping into the water. Swinging through the air on a rope attached to a tree even made the thrill more exciting.

REPRINTED WITH PERMISSION OF THE FLORIDA DEPARTMENT OF CITRUS

Giving a life guard or counselor a toss into the lake was one of the highlights of mischief during summer camp. Quite often by the time that the frolic was finished, everyone had been forced to take a dip, whether they were in their swimming suits or full suit of clothes.

For the more formally inclined adults, an afternoon on the bay in a yacht or fancy sailboat created a relaxing environment that led to dinner and dancing later.

Summer Fun

On the beach

A day at the beach wasn't complete without a picnic basket full of homemade goodies and a sail boat ride with a favorite someone.

FAMOUS BIRTHDAYS

Roger Taylor, July 26

English rock musician of Queen

A quick escape from life's busy schedule was a walk in the sand. These spontaneous moments were sometimes the best time spent together.

A toy boat attached to a rope was a big part of the fun for children spending the day at the beach with their families. Often, boats had been handmade by family members looking forward to the outing.

1949 SEPS

Everyday Life

A night out

Going out for the evening often involved attending community musical and theater presentations as well as neighborhood gatherings. Local families would often gather with their instruments to sing and socialize. Often, homemade snacks were a big part of the get-together.

The formal gatherings still featured the long dresses and styles of the time, with guys wearing their hair slicked back off their ears and women often putting their hair up in buns with decorative barrettes.

Even in formal wear, there was a trend toward more casual and comfortable dress. Low necklines and short sleeves were accompanied by necklaces, bracelets and earrings.

Neighbors and friends often brought their own instruments for an informal evening of singing and dancing. Dress for the occasions continued to become more informal and relaxed.

Casual dress, charming jewelry and that special touch all played their part in melting the hearts of crusty guys, softened to taking off their hat and settling in for moments of love.

Certain looks and even a special song on the piano were ways of passing on feelings to the man of her dreams. Women with musical ability liked to sing and play songs they knew would win the hearts of their intended lover.

The Charm of a Woman

An appropriate gesture of warmth and intense concern and interest were ways of breaking through walls when looking for the soft heart of a man. A woman would often express hints of her intentions by the wearing of jewelry, certain hairstyles and by decorating her hair with flowers or giving inviting looks.

Some women illustrated the old adage, "the way to a man's heart is through his stomach," by cooking special meals or preparing what she understood to be his favorite foods. Others patiently wooed their intended prospects through caring mannerisms and inviting looks at local social outings.

Women loved to pass on their heartfelt feelings with a captivating look and by running their hands through the slicked-back hairstyle of the time.

Everyday Life

Romance

Concepts of romance reached well beyond formal settings to places of the heart. Earlier expectations of fancy dress gave way to casual settings geared toward connecting interest with heart experiences. Memories were made on golf courses, walks in the park, playing ball in the backyard or a trip to the zoo. Boundaries of expectation were broken by casual outings that enabled couples to relax and enjoy each other for who they were.

"Pardon me, but maybe destiny has sat me here."

Looking for wedding rings sometimes brought couples to a new understanding of taste and bargaining personalities. Young men and women sometimes came to grips with a new understanding of the other person's ways of making decisions.

Sporting Life

Baseball

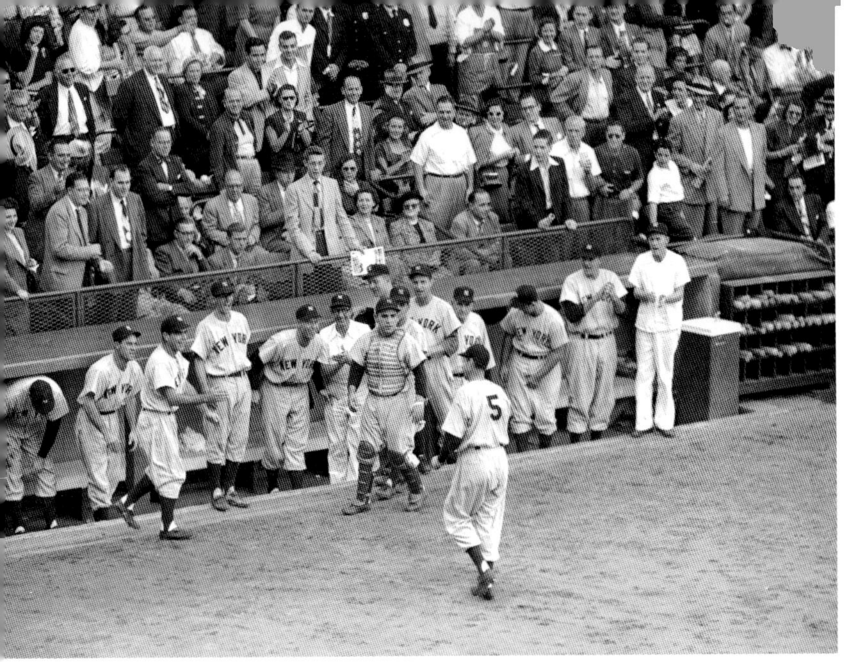

After taking a back seat to the war earlier in the decade, baseball was making an enthusiastic return as Americans returned to the ballpark to once again cheer on their heroes and favorite teams.

After a tight race with Boston, the New York Yankees eliminated the Brooklyn Dodgers in the World Series. One of the members of the Brooklyn squad was Jackie Robinson, baseball's first African American player. Robinson hit .342 to capture the National League batting title while George Kell won the American League title with an average of .343.

Fans bought newspapers just to read about their favorite teams and stadiums began to fill once again as the nation's favorite pastime made a new surge into the hearts of its fans.

New York Yankee teammates come out of the dugout to greet No. 5 Joe DiMaggio after he clouted a homer in one of the 1949 World Series games against the Brooklyn Dodgers at Ebbets Field.

"I'm not *really* mad: This is just for the television audience!"

ELECTRI
20
AT BAT
TEAMS 1 2 3 4 5 6 7
PITTS 0 1 0 0 0 0
BKLYN 0 0 0 0 0
0
BATTING ORDER
Norman Rockwell

© 1949 SEPS
FAMOUS BIRTHDAYS
Shelley Long, August 23
actress
Richard Gere, August 31
actor
JOHN FALTER

Sporting Life

Fishing

Fishing often served as an inexpensive connecting experience between parents and children. Families would often pack sandwiches, fruit and other goodies and head to their favorite fishing hole. Cane poles were still popular but some slightly improved fishing gear was starting to come into its own. Fishing contests awarded those catching the most and largest fish. Fathers and grandfathers often used fishing as a tool to give important life instructions beyond the sport itself to youngsters in the family.

Some found life's greatest enjoyment in taking on a fighting fish in the midst of rapids.

Hip boots and nets were important for those wading into the river behind the old family farm.

"Go tell your daddy there's a man here to see him."

The Metro Daily News FINAL EDITION

AUGUST 29, 1949

THE SOVIET UNION TESTS ITS FIRST ATOMIC BOMB, IGNITING THE ARMS RACE

Sporting Life

Football

Notre Dame was the talk of the nation in college football with an undefeated 10-0 season and a No. 1 ranking. The Fighting Irish were inspired by Heisman Trophy winner Leon Hart and fellow team captain Jim Martin.

In the National Football League, the Philadelphia Eagles outlasted the Los Angeles Rams 14-0 in a championship game held at the Memorial Coliseum in Los Angeles.

With television viewing barely on the horizon, enthusiastic fans followed their favorite teams on the radio or through local media newspaper coverage.

A new type of football helmet and equipment led the way in emphasizing safety. With World War II well behind, fans were turning out to playing fields in full force once again.

Notre Dame's No. 82, Leon Hart goes for the ball during the October 1, 1949 football game against Tulane.

"Second half starts in ten minutes, Mrs. Jones—can you have him patched up by then?"

Everyday Life

A dog's life

The family dog kept things very interesting around the house. With plenty of room to frolic through meadows and open yards, a quick snatch of a baseball by the pup could change one game into another. Trying to corner a dog that has stolen both the baseball and everyone's attention often led to quite a workout.

A frisky young dog found plenty of mischief with which to keep family members busy on the family spread. It was not unusual to find a colorful trail spread by a pup that had explored open paint cans. All of this forced family members to take special measures in cleaning the dog and its evidence.

Children witnessing such scenes often wondered why the pet could seemingly get away with more than they did.

"Just call for me! I'll come."

The companionship of a dog often taught young children the meaning of "man's best friend" and how to cultivate special friendships.

Albert Staehle

NOV
22

"Big fight last night! Mom and I are going to live with grandma!"

"Everybody hang on real tight in case he starts with a sudden jerk!"

"But on the other hand, it might not be full of spiders."

"You go right back in there and come out the right way."

JOHN FALTER

Back to School

Hectic mornings in getting everyone ready to go to school were intensified by large families and the personal touch of home-cooked food. Mothers were up early preparing a full breakfast to make sure that children started out their day with a "full tummy." Most students still carried their lunch pails to school; preparation of bucket meals usually involved sandwiches, fruit, and possibly home-baked goodies such as cookies or brownies.

Looking proper was an important thing so part of the time prior to going to school was consumed in combing hair and making sure clothes and shoes were neat and clean. In addition, everyone was given a homework check before leaving the house.

At school, coats would be hung in the "wrap room" and lunch buckets would be placed on shelves above the coat rack. Once they were settled in, students enjoyed the games designed to teach, such as math races on the blackboard, spelling bees and reading phonetic books aloud. In the midst of the hard work, an errant rubber band, teasing comment or a mischievous remark always made the day more interesting.

1949 WILSON WEAR

© 1949 SEPS

"Teaching me to drive doesn't mean you can tell me what to do.—Ask me to do it!"

1949 USS STEEL

Many children had long walks to school each day. Walking with a best friend made the trip more enjoyable.

© 1949 SEPS

"Listen to this: 'The brown dog walked down the big street.' Is that important enough to be printed in a book?"

Everyday Life

First love

First-love memories were often created in a secret neighborhood clubhouse, school playground or at a picnic following a church's summer vacation Bible School program. Family picnics on the beach or backyard swing sets and sand boxes also served as inviting places for the first little kiss. Sometimes, observing teenagers at the park or in a school play inspired an imitating kiss of young romance, usually secretly away from the awareness of unsuspecting parents.

The intentions of grade school romances were often declared through a class Valentine's Day party or with little notes placed in desks or lockers. Sometimes young lovers would express their youthful romance through giving a piece of candy or other special childhood treat.

1949 JOHNSON & JOHNSON

1949 JOHNSON & JOHNSON

Looking into the eyes of another for the first time is often all that is needed for the first childhood love twinge.

The Metro Daily News

FINAL EDITION

SEPTEMBER 29, 1949

IVA TOGURI D'AQUINO FOUND GUILTY OF BROADCASTING FOR JAPAN

Iva was well known during WWII as "Tokyo Rose."

REPRINTED WITH PERMISSION FROM VALE INCO.

Sitting beside another boy or girl often produced a shyness that gave away special feelings.

School Valentine's parties served as a great opportunity to share special feelings for that classmate who had captured a special place in the heart.

Going to a prom for the first time was always a highlight for a teen-age girl. Shopping for the perfect dress and accessories added to the fun, that created lasting memories.

Everyday Life

Growing up

Improvements in technology and modifications in style changed the way young people expressed themselves. Telephones became more prevalent in talking to friends. Cars became status symbols. The emergence of recorded music introduced new ways of enjoying dance music. Events such as proms and parties led to new ways of dating and exploring friendships.

Expanding horizons in growing into adolescence has always revealed itself in one form or another. The late 1940s opened up trends that would eventually lead to the hot cars and rock music revelations of the next decade.

Hours passed quickly talking to friends on the telephone. Going over the events of the day was so important with a close classmate. Little brothers and sisters would often quietly pick up the phone to find out secrets shared by big sister.

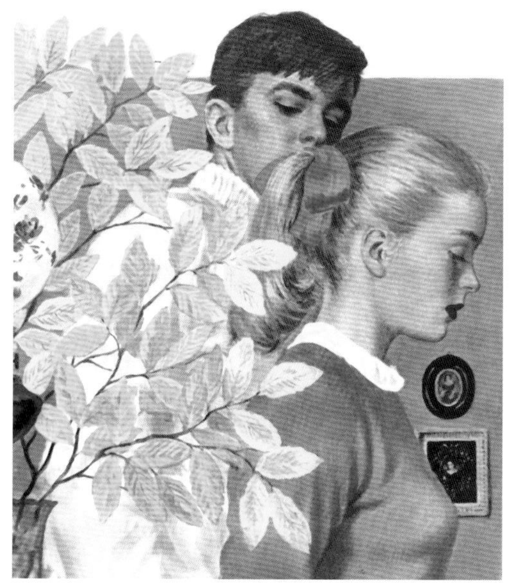

Changing emotions often resulted in seeking opportunities to talk over perceived differences in a quiet living room.

Fathers realized that allowing children to work alongside of them was an educational experience that couldn't be found in textbooks.

Homemade toys made with grandpa's own hands demonstrated love far beyond words to grandchildren.

Grandparents told stories of earlier times that passed family history on to children, who would someday pass the legends on to their own families.

Someone To Look Up To

Family homes with multiple generations provided extra opportunities for role models, especially from grandparents who had plenty of time to invest in grandchildren. Working with a grandpa in building projects or with grandma in household duties gave children the opportunity to learn responsibility and sound thinking. Homes with parents and grandparents working together gave younger family members an extra sense of security and understanding of life as they grew up in an environment of wisdom and faith.

Parents exchanging traditional family roles indicated the importance of family members helping each other, regardless of the job.

Watching experienced elders or grandparents carry out their craftsmanship often planted seeds of creativity in the minds of the young.

British foreign affairs minister Ernest Bevin signs the North Atlantic Treaty during an official ceremony in Washington on April 4, 1949. United States President Harry Truman can be seen in the background.

NATO

World events

The signing of the North Atlantic Treaty on April 4, 1949, established the North Atlantic Treaty Organization (NATO), geared to establish safety and peace for future generations through a united approach to defense.

The treaty was signed in Washington D.C. and included the United States, Canada, and 10 other nations in northern and western Europe. Nations who signed the document agreed that any armed attack against one of its members would be considered an attack against all and would engender a mutual response.

Also in 1949, Ireland severed its last formal tie with the United Kingdom and declared itself to be a republic of its own power.

On April 1, 1949, thousands gathered for the parade for Ireland's independence as it drove past the General Post Office. The nation severed its last formal link with the United Kingdom and declared itself to be a republic. It left the British Commonwealth after having already ceased to participate in that organization for several years

On March 2, 1949, Lucky Lady II, a B-50 Superfortress, landed at Carswell Air Force Base in Fort Worth after a 94-hour flight. The aircraft and crew were participants in the first round-the-world flight as commanded by Captain James Gallagher. The plane flew at an average ground speed of 239 miles per hour.

Cars

Quality and low cost were the primary concerns of those looking to purchase a new car in 1949. Cars competed on the basis of style, color and popular accessories designed to grab the attention of Americans. New and bright colors began to immerge, while different looks were designed to bring character and a sense of celebration to those who were looking for new cars.

1949 STUDEBAKER

Studebaker Land Cruiser

REPRINTED WITH PERMISSION FROM CHRYSLER GROUP, LLC

Hudson

REPRINTED WITH PERMISSION FROM FORD MOTOR COMPANY

Ford Dream Wagon

Plymouth

REPRINTED WITH PERMISSION FROM CHRYSLER GROUP, LLC

The 1949 Plymouth station wagon proved to be the forerunner of Plymouth luxury vehicles that competed for family transportation.

Nash Airflyte

Golden Anniversary Packard Custom

1949 PACKARD

Lincoln Cosmopolitan

DeSoto

What Made Us Laugh

The presence of a racing convertible on a hot summer afternoon brought laughter and bewilderment to those traveling in the more conventional automobiles.

"Look—somebody has to get in the back seat!"

"Teaching me to drive doesn't mean you can tell me what to do.—Ask me to do it!"

"H'm'm'm'm—got your name in for a new car?"

The role of men in car repair was well defined when sweat poured from the forehead of a man attempting to change a tire to the sound of two ladies laughing and waiting to continue their journey. The bewilderment on the man's face fittingly portrays his quiet resentment of the situation.

1949 CHEVROLET

Chevrolet

Cadillac

1949 CADILLAC

Mercury

REPRINTED WITH PERMISSION
FROM FORD MOTOR COMPANY

1949 PONTIAC

Pontiac

Oldsmobile "88"
Convertible Coupe

1949 OLDSMOBILE

Chrysler's silver
anniversary model

REPRINTED WITH PERMISSION
FROM CHRYSLER GROUP, LLC

Buick Rivera

1949 BUICK

Movies

Theaters were entertaining good crowds once again, as such movies as *Samson and Delilah*, *I Was A Male War Bride* and *Twelve O'Clock High* led the popularity charts. Other movies released in 1949 featured the popular comic team of Abbot and Costello.

During the war, many of those with average incomes couldn't afford the luxuries of movie attendance and other social activities. With family members back home and the economy starting to prosper again, Americans were slowly starting to invest in times of pleasure and enjoyment.

Victor Mature and Hedy Lamarr had the leading roles in the No. 1 box office hit, *Samson and Delilah*.

Cary Grant and Ann Sheridan captured the hearts of Americans in the movie, *I Was a Male War Bride*.

Tops at the Box Office

Samson and Delilah
Battleground
Jolson Sings Again
Sands of Iwo Jima
I Was a Male War Bride
Twelve O'Clock High
Pinky
The Heiress
Little Women
All the King's Men
Adam's Rib

Oscar winners for the year included Mercedes McCambridge, supporting actress—*All the King's Men*; Broderick Crawford, best actor—*All the King's Men*; Olivia deHavilland, best actress—*The Heiress* and Dean Jagger, best supporting actor—*Twelve O'Clock High*. Best picture award went to *All the King's Men* and Joseph L. Mankiewicz was awarded best director for his work in *A Letter to Three Wives*.

In *All the King's Men*, Broderick Crawford starred as a politician from a rural county who rose to the governor's mansion. Much of his political journey was a result of self-taught education and political understanding.

Musician Cozy Cole became a well-known backup drummer for the famed Louis Armstrong. Here, Cole is seen in November of 1949 performing with Armstrong at Symphony Hall in Boston.

Improved technology in the record playing industry and 33⅓ rpm records especially, opened a whole new market of sales for musicians of the time. Music that had once been limited to radio was now available to those who purchased record players for their homes.

Dinah Shore, well-known for singing the, "See the USA in your Chevrolet" commercial, made her first television debut on the *Ed Wynn Show*. Her popularity began to rise and she was given her own show, *The Dinah Shore Show*, two years later.

The Metro Daily News

FINAL EDITION

FIVE CENTS

OCTOBER 7, 1949

THE DEMOCRATIC REPUBLIC OF GERMANY IS OFFICIALLY ESTABLISHED

Music

© GETTY IMAGES

Several well-known singers of the 50s and 60s made their debut in 1949, including Mitch Miller, Eddie Fisher and Frankie Laine, shown at right.

Laine was recruited by Miller and the two became one of the most popular hit-making teams of the time. Laine's folk spiritual, "The Lucky Old Sun," caught on immediately as a statement of faith and a working man's hope to bring suffering to an end.

"Mule Train," the musical duo's second hit, proved to be even bigger. At one point, Laine was the first artist to ever hold the number one and number two songs on the chart at the same time.

Other popular hits of the year included, "A—You're Adorable," by Perry Como, "Baby, it's Cold Outside" by Dinah Shore and Buddy Clark, and "Dear Hearts and Gentle People," recorded both by Bing Crosby and Ralph Flanagan.

Marked improvement in the record industry allowed for musicians to begin sharing their music on a more widespread scale to an entirely new market of fans.

REPRINTED WITH PERMISSION OF TECHNICOLOR

Top Hits of 1949

"Ghost Riders in the Sky"
Vaughn Monroe

"That Lucky Old Sun"
Frankie Laine

"A Little Bird Told Me"
Evelyn Knight & The Stardusters

"Cruising Down the River"
Russ Morgan & His Orchestra

"Mule Train"
Frankie Laine

"Some Enchanted Evening"
Perry Como

"You're Breaking My Heart"
Vic Damone

"Cruising Down the River"
Blue Barron

"All I Want for Christmas Is My Two Front Teeth"
Spike Jones

"Buttons and Bows"
Dinah Shore

Transportation

Over land and over sea

The possibility of the middle class affording mass transportation opened the opportunity for many who had never flown before as they took plane trips, enjoyed scenic train rides and took tourist cruises.

National airlines competing for business from travelers offered packages designed to invite those who were in tight financial circumstances. Trains rolled through mountain passes and along scenic rivers, while boats transported people to remote hiking and swimming opportunities.

Heading to the beach became a more frequent summer routine for those needing to get away from home.

Train cars designed with complete living quarters became attractive to those with children who had never seen mountains or other parts of the country.

FAMOUS BIRTHDAYS

Bonnie Raitt, November 8
country singer and guitarist

Paul Shaffer, November 28
Canadian-American musician of *Late Night With David Letterman*

1949 PAN AMERICAN

1949 CALIFORINA ZEPHYR

Breathtaking scenery awaited those who traveled into such areas as the Rocky and Smokey Mountains. Railroads were built around mountains and streams in a fashion that gave them the sensation of clinging to the sides of the mountains.

paradise of the pacific
SWIMMING
FISHING
SUNBATHING
CALIFORNIA
MEXICO
ACAPULCO
WONDER TOUR
OUTGOING
INCOMING
alajalov

Seeing the World

A nation that had been confined financially by the war began to move out to visit other parts of the world following World War II. Improvements in transportation opened the door to travel to sites once thought unimaginable. Americans began to enjoy seasonal differences in other parts of the world by traveling to warm climates during the dead of winter in the northern regions.

Travel agencies became an expanding business in assisting travelers with the hottest travel spots and best prices. Other individuals took time to visit far-away relatives that they once thought they might never see again.

1949 SOUTHERN PACIFIC

Such sites as mountains mirrored in beautiful lakes was only a picture or calendar view to most Americans prior to scenic train rides traveling across the U.S.

1949 PAN AMERICAN

Dining outdoors in the midst of winter, dressed in summer clothes, was a new experience for those who traveled to such spots as the West Indies or southern Florida.

1949 PAN AMERICAN

A plane ride to Rio only took 27 hours from United States departure points. Plane advertisements boasted relaxing sleeping arrangements on longer flights.

1949 SEPS

1949 TWA

Improved transportation opportunities made it possible for generational family mergings.

1949 AMERICAN AIRLINES

Transportation

Families on the go

The return of all family members from the war and an improving post-war economy made it possible for travel opportunities to expand. Many who had never been farther than several miles from their home had opportunities to visit relatives in different parts of the country by car, plane and train. Even locally, recreational trips occurred more frequently.

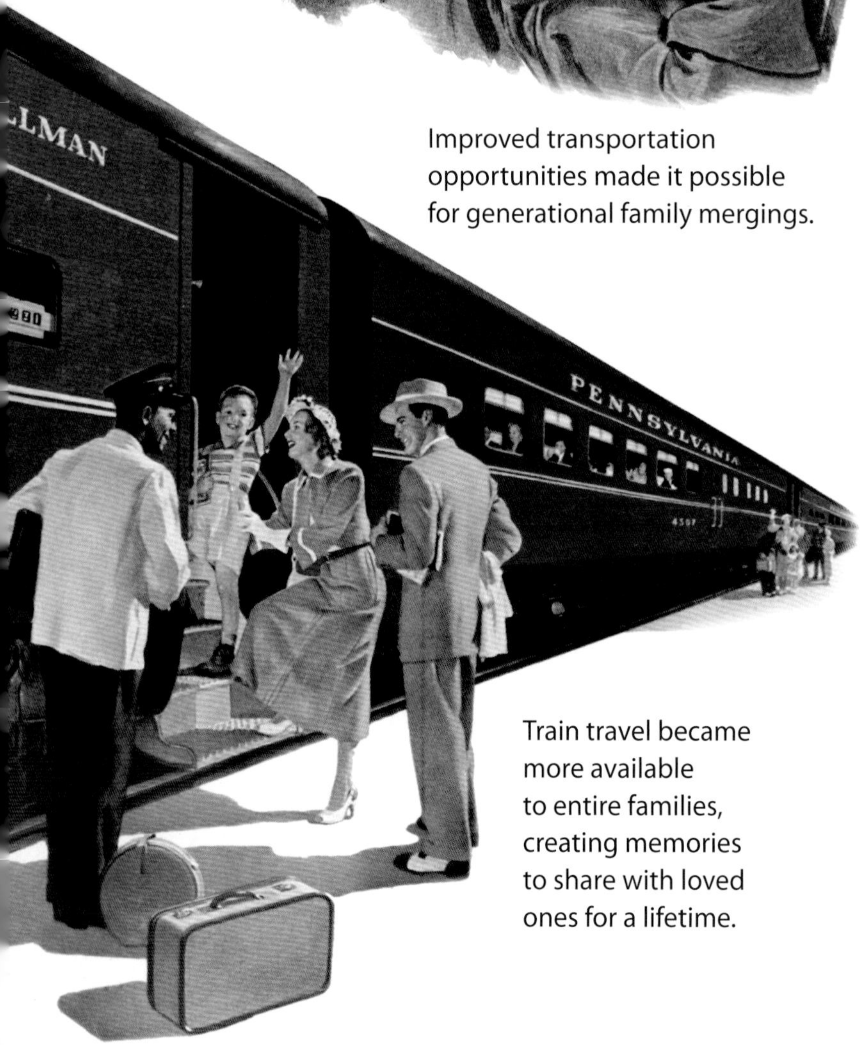

Train travel became more available to entire families, creating memories to share with loved ones for a lifetime.

1949 PENNSYLVANIA RAILROAD

1949 AMERICAN AIRLINES

More affordable plane flights created family reunions that wouldn't have occurred otherwise.

Stevan Dohanos

What Made Us Laugh

© 1949 SEPS

"What's the matter with him, lady? Is he sick?"

© 1949 SEPS

"I never forget a face … aren't you the man who took my order?"

© 1949 SEPS

"NEXT!"

© 1949 SEPS

"Hey, mister."

"Not 'Boithday,' young man. It's 'Happy Birthday, Birthday.' Now let's try it again."

"THERE you are, honey! I've been looking all over town for you!

"Don't get coy with me, Elinor—you know Per-feetly well what those background noises are!"

Good hearing was essential to pick up "over the shoulder" tidbits that were being given in small town cafes.

Everyday Life

Shopping and dining

The personal touch of neighborhood shops provided families with local social experiences and quality service. Downtown stores would often stay open later on Friday and Saturday evenings in order to accommodate grocery lists and personal retail needs.

Store owners often kept items in stock for certain customers they knew would need them. Many people had ongoing accounts at certain stores; there was no problem with credit because each trusted the other and knew that financial matters would be taken care of.

Some downtown communities would have band concerts or dances on downtown streets on the weekend to provide entertainment for shoppers. In addition, businesses would often provide treats for children. Malls and large shopping centers were still years in the future.

1949 GENERAL ELECTRIC COMPANY

Needs of all kinds and many luxuries were available. Most residents only left town to visit large communities at special times such as Christmas or for occasional family outings.

© LIBRARY OF CONGRESS, PRINTS AND PHOTOGRAPHS DIVISION, GSC 5A16374

© LIBRARY OF CONGRESS, PRINTS AND PHOTOGRAPHS DIVISION, GSC 5A16374

The local clothing store helped shape the trends in the community. Neighbors would often see certain clothing worn by someone in church and would seek out a similar garment the next week.

The Metro Daily News

FINAL EDITION

NOVEMBER 24, 1949

SQUAW VALLEY SKI RESORT OPENS IN CALIFORNIA

REPRINTED WITH PERMISSION OF DU PONT

1949 CONTINENTAL OIL COMPANY

Parents would take the time to play alongside their children in constructing snow-made items. Everything from snowmen to igloos were projects enjoyed by family members having fun together.

© 1949 SEPS

Winter Scenes

While large cities sported professional looking skating rinks as part of their winter tradition, such scenes in local and small communities occurred in creative locations. Farm ponds and community parks served as gathering places for winter activities on cold, snowy afternoons. Parents and children would join together to skate, sled and make snow figures. Often, those participating would bring hot chocolate and homemade goodies to go along with the winter frolic.

Winter Scenes

Snowstorms were often days to snuggle in with family members and enjoy the spoils of hard work. There was plenty of food stored and cupboards were full of goodies for family baking projects. It was also a time to catch up on reading and enjoying family group games around the dining room table.

Chores such as carrying wood and coal to the house were accepted responsibilities among family members. Restless boys eager to get out of the house often found satisfaction in harvesting wood that had been cut for winter use.

John Clymer

The Night Before Christmas

Many families spent the final few hours before Christmas decorating the family tree. Many ornaments were homemade or special gifts that had been passed down through generations. Hand prints and homemade school trinkets hung on the tree as a reminder of days when adults once shared the childhood creativity of youthful Christmas. Some wreaths had been made by grandparents. Personalized gifts from former Christmases brought back memories of years past.

For many, the night before Christmas also consisted of choir concerts, Christmas worship and various festive instrumental musical presentations. In northern settings howling winds and snowstorms often added a bit of romance to the occasion.

"Incidentally ... you get around; have conditions in foreign lands shown an appreciable return to postwar normalcy?"

Unpacking family heirlooms to decorate the family tree often created an opportunity to pass down generations of Christmas stories to inquisitive children. It proved to be a time of bonding and connectedness between generations.

The Spirit of Christmas

The appearance of Santa Claus at the local department store was a main attraction for children as parents completed last minute Christmas shopping. Getting to sit on Santa's lap and sharing their wish list was the ultimate joy for each girl and boy.

The Bible account of the Christmas story was still the heart of Christmas celebration. Family gatherings would be planned surrounding the program, which featured children and grandchildren. Christmas treats would add to the joyful festivities as worshipers walked into the wintry night singing and laughing.

; the big children were worse than the small ones ne to snooping for presents. Here, a wife discovers her gift to her in the closet and shakes it to see if it contains r jewelry.

in 1949

Pen sets were one of the most popular gifts and were often the envy of those looking on with thos fortunate enough to receive one.

"Mind if I play with your gifts?"

The sight of Christmas toys often brought back memories to adults reflecting on their own childhood Christmases. Often, the little child within would motivate older family members to join in playing with children. At times, the adults were interested in the new toys longer than the youngsters.

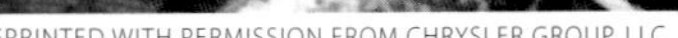

The excitement of Christmas morning is shown as the young daughter wraps her arms around Mom as she thanks both parents for her gifts.

THE SATURDAY EVENING
POST
JANUARY 1, 1949 15¢
THEY ASK TO BE KILLED
By David G. Wittels
CLEVELAND, OHIO
A Dairyman Admits: Milk Costs Too Much

More *The Saturday Evening Post* Covers

The Saturday Evening Post covers were works of art, many illustrated by famous artists of the time, including Norman Rockwell. Most of the 1949 covers have been incorporated within the previous pages of this book; the few that were not are presented on the following pages for your enjoyment.

THE SATURDAY EVENING
POST
JANUARY 8, 1949 15¢
THE U-BOAT MYSTERY OF SCAPA FLOW
By Burke Wilkinson
I Was Blind But Now I See
By Major Robert P. Steptoe

THE SATURDAY EVENING
POST
JANUARY 15, 1949 15¢
WHAT THE COAL MINERS SAY ABOUT JOHN L. LEWIS
By John Bartlow Martin
A New Leslie Ford Mystery

All Europe is on our Side of the Question, as far as Applause and good Wishes can carry them. ~~ Those who live under arbitrary Power do nevertheless approve of Liberty, and wish for it; they almost despair of recovering it in Europe; ~~~~'tis a Common Observation here, that our Cause is *the Cause of all Mankind*, and that we are fighting for their Liberty in defending our own.

Benj. Franklin 1777

© 1949 SEPS

© 1949 SEPS

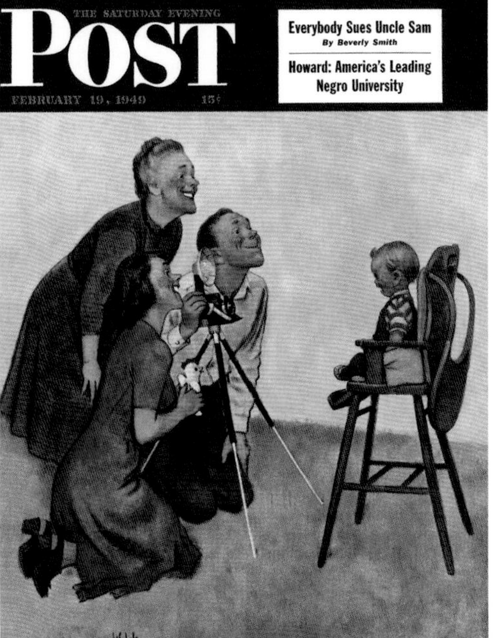

© 1949 SEPS

THE SATURDAY EVENING
POST
APRIL 2, 1949
15¢
GOVERNOR STEVENSON:
REBEL IN ILLINOIS
By Joe Alex Morris
I Went Out With the Trawlers
By Charles Rawlings
HOW RUSSIAN CHILDREN
LOST THEIR GOD
By Nina Alexeieva
Albert Staehle

THE SATURDAY EVENING
POST
APRIL 30, 1949
15¢
How Our Foreign Policy is Made
By Joseph and Stewart Alsop
WHAT YOU CAN BELIEVE
ABOUT FLYING SAUCERS
By Sidney Shalett

THE SATURDAY EVENING
POST
MAY 28, 1949
15¢
I Learned About Communism
the Hard Way
By PAUL RUEDEMANN
NEW HAVEN:
Yale's Home Town

THE SATURDAY EVENING
POST
JULY 2, 1949
15¢
WASHINGTON'S GREATEST STORYTELLER
Advance, Mr. Hornblower!
By C. S. Forester
I Saw Russia Preparing for War
By Nicholas Nyaradi
EX-FINANCE MINISTER OF HUNGARY

THE SATURDAY EVENING
POST
JULY 30, 1949
15¢
Moscow's Phony Peace Campaign
By Demaree Bess
CHATTANOOGA

THE SATURDAY EVENING
POST
SEPTEMBER 10, 1949
15¢
A Federal Agent Tells His Story:
I WAS A WIRE TAPPER
OMAHA
WHAT SHALL WE DO ABOUT COMMUNIST TEACHERS?
BUS STOP

MADISON AVENUE COACH
183

BUS STOP

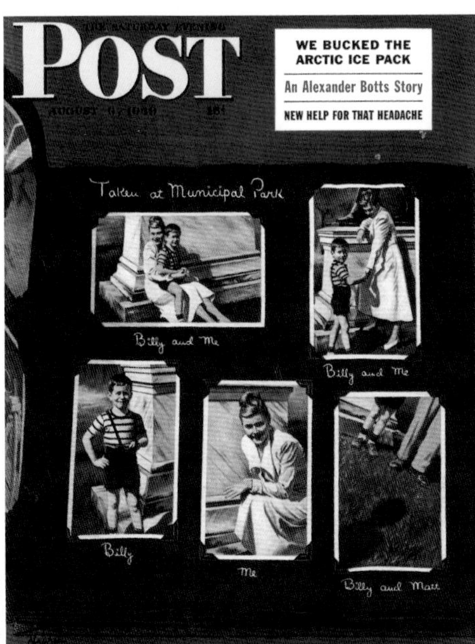
POST
WE BUCKED THE ARCTIC ICE PACK
An Alexander Botts Story
NEW HELP FOR THAT HEADACHE
Taken at Municipal Park
Billy and Me
Billy and Me
Billy
Me
Billy and Matt

January 2
Christopher Durang, playwright

January 15
Howard Allen Twitty, PGA golfer

January 17
Andy Kaufman, comedian and actor
Michael Kevin "Mick" Taylor, English musician

January 22
Steve Perry, singer
Mike Caldwell, baseball player

January 23
Robert D. Cabana, astronaut

January 30
Peter Agre, biologist and recipient of the Nobel Prize in Chemistry

February 1
Jimmy Lee Thorpe, PGA golfer

February 5
Kurt Beck, German politician

February 10
Joe Lavender, NFL player

February 15
Ken Anderson, NFL quarterback

February 20
Ivana Trump, Czech business woman

March 3
James S. Voss, astronaut

March 12
Rob Cohen, film director, producer and writer

March 13
Julia Migenes, soprano

March 16
Elliott Murphy, singer/songwriter

March 17
Patrick Duffy, actor

March 21
Eddie Money, singer/guitarist

March 28
Ronnie Ray Smith, 4 X 100m relay runner

March 29
Michael Brecker, jazz musician

March 30
Naomi Sims, model and businesswomen

April 3
Richard Thompson, English musician and songwriter

April 8
Philip Aaberg, jazz keyboardist and composer

April 18
Geoff Bodine, race car driver

April 22
Judith Arlene Resnik, astronaut
Spencer Haywood, NBA player

April 23
Joyce DeWitt, actress

April 26
Jerry Blackwell, wrestler

May 4
John Force, race car driver

May 13
Zoë Wanamaker, British-American actress

May 16
Rick Reuschel, baseball pitcher

May 20
Dave Thomas, Canadian actor and comedian

May 23
Alan Garcia, President of Peru

May 26
Philip Michael Thomas, actor
Dan Pastorini, NFL quarterback

May 29
Francis Rossi, English rock guitarist and singer

May 31
Tom Berenger, actor

June 2
Heather Couper, British astronomer

June 8
Andrew Lees, British scientist and environmentalist

June 11
Frank Beard, rock musician

June 22
Alan Osmond, singer

June 25
Phyllis George-Brown, Miss America 1971

June 27
Vera Wang, fashion designer

June 28
Don Baylor, baseball player

June 29
Dan Dierdorf, NFL player & sportscaster

July 2
David Eaton, composer, conductor and producer

July 3
Johnnie Wilder, Jr., vocalist

July 7
Shelley Duvall, actress

July 8
Wolfgang Puck, Austrian chef

July 17
Charlie Steiner, sportscaster

July 26
Thaksin Shinawatra, Thai businessman and former Prime Minister

July 29
Marilyn Quayle, wife of vice president Dan Quayle

August 4
John Riggins, football player

August 8
Keith Carradine, actor

August 15
Beverly Lynn Burns, pilot and first woman in the world to captain the Boeing 747

August 20
Philip Lynott, Irish rock musician

August 21
Loretta Devine, actress

August 23
Rick Springfield, Australian rock singer and actor

August 25
Gene Simmons, Israeli-American hard rock bass guitarist and singer

August 31
H. David Politzer, physicist, Nobel Prize laureate

September 4
Tom Watson, PGA golfer

September 9
John Curry, British figure skater
Joe Theismann, NFL quarterback
Susilo Bambang Yudhoyono, President of Indonesia

September 11
Bill Whittington, race car driver

September 18
Peter Shilton, English footballer

September 22
Harold Carmichael, NFL wide receiver

September 26
Jane Smiley, novelist

September 27
Mike Schmidt, baseball player

October 5
Bill James, baseball writer

October 13
Tom Mees, sports broadcaster

October 17
Bill Hudson, musician

October 21
Benjamin Netanyahu, Prime Minister of Israel

October 24
Nick Ainger, politician

October 25
Réjean Houle, Canadian ice hockey player

October 26
Juanin Clay, actress

October 28
Bruce Jenner, decathlete and Olympic winner
Ronnie Mund, television personality

November 3
Larry Holmes, world heavyweight champion
Anna Wintour, English-American editor and journalist

November 5
Jimmie Spheeris, singer-songwriter

November 19
Ahmad Rashad, sportscaster and television personality

November 25
Kerry James O'Keeffe, Australian cricketer and commentator

December 4
Jeff Bridges, actor

December 7
T**om Waits,** singer, composer, and actor

December 8
Mary Gordon, writer

December 13
Randy Owen, country lead vocalist, rhythm guitar player

December 22
Maurice and Robin Gibb, British rock musicians

December 25
Sissy Spacek, actress
Joe Louis Walker, musician

Facts and Figures of 1949

President of the U.S.
Harry S. Truman
Vice President of the U.S.
Alben W. Barkley

Population of the U. S.
149,200,000
Births
3,649,000

High School Graduates
Males: 571,000
Females: 629,000

U.S. ARMY, COURTESY OF HARRY S. TRUMAN LIBRARY

Average Salary for full-time employee: $3037.00
Minimum Wage (per hour): $0.40

Average cost for:

Item	Cost
Bread (lb.)	$0.14
Bacon (lb.)	$0.66
Butter (lb.)	$0.72
Eggs (doz.)	$0.69
Milk (gal.)	$0.42
Potatoes (10 lbs.)	$0.54
Coffee (lb.)	$0.55
Sugar (5 lb.)	$0.47
Gasoline (gal.)	$0.26
Movie Ticket	$0.46
Postage Stamp	$0.03
Car	$1,650.00
Single-Family home	$ 7,450.00

REPRINTED WITH PERMISSION FROM FORD MOTOR COMPANY

Notable Inventions and Firsts

January 17: The first Volkswagen Beetle arrived in the U.S. by Dutch businessman Ben Pon. Only two 1949 models were sold in the U.S. that year.

January 25: In the first Israeli election, David Ben-Gurion becomes Prime Minister.

January 31: The first TV daytime soap opera, *These Are My Children,* was broadcast from the NBC station in Chicago.

February 7: Joe DiMaggio becomes the first baseball player to earn $100,000 a year.

March 20: The Chicago, Burlington & Quincy, Denver & Rio Grande, Western and Western Pacific railroads inaugurate the California Zephyr passenger train between Chicago and Oakland, California, as the first long-distance train to feature Vista Dome cars as regular equipment.

April 7: Rodgers and Hammerstein's *South Pacific*, starring Mary Martin and Ezio Pinza, opens on Broadway and goes on to become R & H's second longest running musical.

May 1: Nereid, a moon of Neptune, is discovered by Gerard P. Kuiper.

June 24: The first television western, *Hopalong Cassidy*, airs on NBC.

July 7: *Dragnet* airs for the first time on NBC radio with actor Jack Webb as Sgt. Joe Friday.

October 1: People's Republic of China proclaimed at Beijing with Mao Tse-tung as chairman.

November 25: "Rudolf, the Red-Nosed Reindeer" appeared on the music charts. It was originally an advertising jingle.

December 8: *Blondes* opens on Broadway at the Ziegfeld Theatre and runs for 740 performance.

Silly Putty is introduced by New Haven, Conn., advertising man Peter C.L. Hodgson.

General Mills and Pillsbury introduce prepared cake mixes, initially in chocolate, gold and white varieties.

Sara Lee Cheese Cake is introduced by Chicago baker Charles Lubin, 44.

Sports Winners

World Series: New York Yankees defeat Brooklyn Dodgers

Stanley Cup: Toronto Maple Leafs defeat Detroit Red Wings

NFL: Philadelphia Eagles defeat Los Angeles Rams

The Masters: Sam Snead wins

PGA Championship: Sam Snead wins

NBA: Minneapolis Lakers defeat Washington Capitols

Live It Again 1949

PROJECT EDITOR	Barb Sprunger
ART DIRECTOR	Brad Snow
COPYWRITER	Jim Langham
EDITORIAL ASSISTANT	Stephanie Smith
PRODUCTION ARTIST SUPERVISOR	Erin Augsburger
PRODUCTION ARTIST	Erin Augsburger
COPY EDITORS	Emily Carter, Amanda Scheerer
PHOTOGRAPHY SUPERVISOR	Tammy Christian
NOSTALGIA EDITOR	Ken Tate
EDITORIAL DIRECTOR	Jeanne Stauffer
PUBLISHING SERVICES DIRECTOR	Brenda Gallmeyer

Printed in China
First Printing: 2010
Library of Congress Number: 2009904232
ISBN: 978-1-59635-278-0

Customer Service
LiveItAgain.com
(800) 829-5865

We would like to thank Curtis Publishing for the art prints used in this book. For fine-art prints and more information on the artists featured in *Live It Again 1949* contact Curtis Publishing, Indianapolis, IN 46202, (317) 633-2070, All rights reserved, www.curtispublishing.com

We would like to acknowledge and thank the HMX Group, the owner of the Hart Schaffner Marx trademark.

We would like to thank the Wisconsin Historical Society for the use of their online Photograph and Image collection (www.wisconsinhistory.org) and CNH America LLC.

1 2 3 4 5 6 7 8 9